The Poles

Greg Nickles

CRABTREE
Publishing Company
www.crabtreebooks.com

CRABTREE
Publishing Company

PMB 16A, 350 Fifth Avenue
Suite 3308
New York, NY 10118

612 Welland Avenue
St. Catharines, Ontario
L2M 5V6

Co-ordinating editor: Ellen Rodger
Content editor: Kate Calder
Production co-ordinator: Rosie Gowsell
Assistant editor: Lisa Gurusinghe

Prepress: Embassy Graphics
Printer: Worzalla Publishing Company

Created by: Brown Partworks Ltd.
Commissioning editor: Anne O'Daly
Project editor: Clare Oliver
Picture researcher: Adrian Bentley
Designer: Matthew Greenfield
Maps: Mark Walker
Consultant: Professor Donald Avery, Ph.D. History

CATALOGING-IN-PUBLICATION DATA
Nickles, Greg, 1969-
    The Poles / Greg Nickles.
    p.cm. – (We came to North America)
    Includes index.
    ISBN 0-7787-0192-1 (RLB) – ISBN 0-7787-0206-5 (pbk.)
    1. Polish Americans–History–Juvenile literature. 2. Polish Americans–Biography–Juvenile literature. 3. Polish Americans–Social life and customs–Juvenile literature [1. Polish Americans–History]   I. Series
    E184.P7 N54 2001
    973'.049185–dc21
                    00-069357
                    LC

Photographs
AKG London 5 (bottom), 7 (bottom), 13 (bottom). AP Photo Gino Domenico 28 (top). The Art Archive 11 (top); Chopin Foundation, Warsaw/Dagli Orti 26 (top). Brown Partworks 9; National Archives 17 (bottom), 30 (top). Corbis David Turnley 25 (top); Historical Picture Archive 7 (top); James L. Amos 19 (top); Kelly-Mooney Photography front cover, 26 (bottom); Lake County Museum 24 (top); Ray Krantz 21; Sandy Felsenthal 16, 19 (bottom), 27 (top). EMPICS Tony Marshall 31 (bottom). Glenbow Archives, Calgary, Canada (NA-3091-83) 17 (top); (NA-3091-86) 25 (bottom); (NA-3091-66) 29 (top). Hulton Getty title page, 4, 5 (top), 6, 10, 15, 18, 23 (top). Image Bank Archive Photos 13 (top). Kobal Collection 30 (bottom). Mary Evans Picture Library 12. Panna Maria Historical Society, Panna Maria, Texas 11 (bottom). Polish American Cultural Center Museum, Philadelphia 24 (bottom), 27 (bottom). Polish Information Agency, Warsaw 29 (bottom). Polish Museum of America, Chicago 28 (bottom). Robert Hunt Library 22, 23 (bottom). Ronald Grant Archive 31 (top).

Cover: Dancers with the Matusz Polish Dance Circle wear traditional costumes at a Polish Festival in Holmdel, New Jersey.

Book Credits
Library of Congress, Manuscript Division, WPA Federal Writers' Project Collection.

Contents

Introduction

Today, almost ten million people in the United States and more than 250,000 in Canada share Polish **ancestry**. Some are the **descendants** of Poles who **immigrated** centuries ago. Others arrived more recently, and more immigrate each year.

Poles have been immigrating from Poland to North America since 1608. The earliest arrivals were tradespeople, who helped the first British settlers. Later, Poles took factory jobs in the rapidly growing cities, although most had been farmers in their home country. Today, Poles and their descendants work in just about every type of job.

Poland's history stretches back more than a thousand years. In the last 250 years, Poland has suffered devastating wars. The countries that defeated Poland did not stop at robbing the Poles of their land and wealth. They often tried to wipe out the Polish **culture** and people, too.

As these troubles took their toll, the number of people who left Poland soared from thousands to millions. Most Poles who came to North America, immigrated between the 1870s and the beginning of World War I (1914–1918). More Poles arrived after World War II (1939-1945) and since the 1980s.

▼ The Polish hero, Thaddeus Kosciusko, (center) led the Polish uprising of 1794. The Poles were rebelling against Prussian and Russian control of their homeland.

Christianity and Judaism

Most Polish immigrants belonged to one of two religions: **Christianity** and **Judaism**. The vast majority of Polish immigrants were Christians, people who follow the teachings of Jesus Christ. Most Polish Christians belonged to the **Roman Catholic Church**, which is led by the **Pope**, who lives in the Vatican in Rome, Italy. Judaism is an ancient religion based upon the teachings of a holy book called the Torah. Most Jews, or followers of Judaism, immigrated to North America in the mid-1900s.

▲ The Pope is the head of the Roman Catholic Church. Pope John Paul II is Polish. He was born at Wadowice, Poland, in 1920.

The attacks against Polish culture in Europe have led Poles in North America to work hard to **preserve** their traditions. Many continue to speak and write the Polish language, and teach their children Polish history. They have parades that celebrate community pride, and, at special events or during holidays, people eat traditional Polish foods or dance to Polish polka music. For many Poles, a strong devotion to the Roman Catholic Church is also an important part of preserving Polish culture.

The lives of Poles in North America have been better than in Poland during its hard times. Nevertheless, Poles and their descendants have had to overcome many challenges, including poverty and **prejudice** in school, at work, and in their neighborhoods. Today, they proudly hold on to their Polish culture and identities.

▼ Poles board a ship bound for the United States from Southampton, England, in 1921.

A Proud Heritage

Located in the center of Europe, Poland is a large country of forests, lakes, and *fertile* plains. Over the thousand years since its birth, Poland has often struggled with its neighbors over control of its land.

Historians believe that the Poles first moved to the land that is now called Poland around 500 A.D. One Slavic tribe was called the Polanie, which means plain dwellers. They took their name from the pola, or open fields.

The first powerful Polish territory was created around 900 A.D. by Mieszko I. He led the Poles to victory in battles with neighboring nations. Most Poles regard 966 A.D. as the year that their nation, which they call *Polska*, was born. It was then that Mieszko became a member of the Roman Catholic Church and encouraged his **subjects** to **convert**. The Church had a strong influence on the growing kingdom. It brought scholars who taught Christianity as well as **literacy**, politics, and science. The Church also linked Poland to other Roman Catholic countries, some of which became powerful **allies**.

Despite years of wars with other kingdoms and struggles among its own people, by the 1300s, Poland became a strong power. It developed close ties with Italy, whose thriving culture influenced Polish scholars and artists. Science and the arts flourished in Poland.

▲ Despite the wealth of their rulers and noble families, most ordinary Poles were peasant farmers.

6

◄ **Mieszko I ruled Poland from about 963 A.D. until his death in 992 A.D.**

At a time when thousands of Europeans were punished if they were of an unfavored nation or religion, Poland gained a reputation for accepting people of many backgrounds, including many Jews.

The wealth Poland earned from its growing trade was reflected in the country's castles, cathedrals, and universities. Unfortunately, only noble families had the luxury of gaining an education. Most Poles remained poor and never went to school.

Poland's strength and success did not last. As the centuries passed, the country suffered damaging attacks, especially from the kingdoms of Prussia, Austria, and Russia. These neighbors overtook more and more of Poland until the entire country was taken over by the end of the 1700s. The Poles remained under foreign rule until the mid-1900s.

▲ **The Polish capital, Warsaw, was invaded by the Prussians in 1655, by the Russians in 1794, by the Germans in 1939, and again by the Russians in 1944.**

◄ **This painting shows a scene from the Polish Revolution of 1830 to 1831. At this time, Poland was controlled by the Russian czar, Nicholas I. This Polish uprising failed and the czar made Poland part of the Russian Empire.**

Eyewitness to History

MRS. WALTER PINKUS was born near Tarnov, Poland, in 1864. She and her husband were poor farmers who worked day and night to make enough money to survive. They *emigrated* to the United States in 1893. She recalls how hard it was to make a living in Poland.

"My husband received the farm from the [landlord], and, as pay for this land (about six acres), my husband agreed to work for the [landlord] three days per week for so many years. In this time, the land would be paid for. What would happen if he didn't go? He would be brought in court and charged with **misdemeanor**. The **sentence** would probably be so many strikes with a whip.

We were too poor to have any horses, and the heavy work on our farm had to be done by people who had. In return, we had to pay them back by working ourselves.

Because of this, and the agreement with the [landlord], we had to be away working for someone else during the day, and the work on our farm had to be done mostly at night. Many times I took my little baby into the field with me and kept working, taking care of it as best I could. This did not seem unusual because everyone had to do the same, but, now, as one looks back, it seems almost impossible."

Early Polish Settlers

In 1608, several Polish tradespeople **disembarked** from the ships, *Mary* and *Margaret*, at Jamestown, in the new English **colony** of Virginia. They were the first of a small but steady number of Poles, who settled in North America in the 1600s, 1700s, and early 1800s.

The founders of Jamestown wanted to make goods to trade in English markets. Glass was in great demand, and several Polish glassmakers were invited to Jamestown in 1608. Their knowledge, hard work, and skill as soldiers impressed the English, who invited many more to live in their colonies.

In 1619, Poles in Virginia went on **strike** to demand a fair voice in the colony's government. The English recognized their importance by giving them the same rights as the English settlers. The Poles' strike is often celebrated as the first civil rights protest in U.S. history.

▼ Sailing ships brought more Polish settlers and fresh **provisions** to Jamestown in 1610.

A stream of Polish immigrants flowed into North America from the 1600s. The first were tradespeople, farmers, and laborers. Later, wealthy Poles arrived, including nobles, landowners, and professional soldiers. Casimir Pulaski was a Polish nobleman and soldier who came to North America in 1777. He became a hero in the fight for America's independence from Britain in the War of Independence (1775–1783). He died at the Siege of Savannah in 1779.

▲ Some Polish immigrants were lured west by California's Gold Rush in 1849.

In 1854, a group of Poles led by Father Leopold Moczygemba moved to Texas and founded the town of Panna Maria, which is Polish for "Virgin Mary." The townspeople faced difficulties, including prejudice from other settlers, attacks by outlaws, disease, deadly snakes, and even plagues of grasshoppers. Despite this, they established North America's first Polish school and church, and encouraged the founding of other Polish settlements.

Very few Poles immigrated to Canada before the mid-1800s. By the 1870s, the Polish community in Canada had only about 600 people. Most of these Polish immigrants lived in Montréal, Québec, and Ontario. In the late 1800s, Canada's first Polish farming community was founded at Barry's Bay, Ontario.

▼ Father Moczygemba founded Panna Maria, Texas, in 1854. It was North America's first all-Polish settlement.

Jan of Kolno

Polish histories tell of a Pole named Jan of Kolno, who may have sailed to North America in 1476, many years before Christopher Columbus' famous first voyage of 1492.

The accounts say that Jan reached Labrador, Canada, and followed the east coast as far south as the Delaware River. Unfortunately, Jan died on the return trip, so no one can be sure of the details of his story.

The Journey

Leaving their homeland was a difficult choice for the millions of Poles who emigrated between the 1870s and World War I (1914–1918). Polish travelers faced a long journey from their tiny, rural villages across the Atlantic Ocean, to the busy cities of North America.

The second half of the 1800s were troubled times for the people of Poland. The Prussians, Austrians, and Russians, who had ruled their land since the late 1700s stopped most Poles from owning land or businesses, or from gaining political power. Most people lived in poverty. Thousands of others were unfairly imprisoned, especially middle-class Poles who had taken part in the rebellious uprisings of 1830 and 1848. Polish culture was under attack. In parts of the land, the Polish language was banned, churches taken over, and Polish leaders cast out or **executed**.

Rather than face poverty and live under foreign control in Poland, many Poles looked to the outside world. They were encouraged to move to North America by letters from friends who were already there and by advertisements. The United States had a reputation for offering well-paid jobs and inexpensive land to immigrants. The freedoms of speech and worship enjoyed there also appealed to the suffering Poles.

▼ Emigrants wait for a ship that will take them to their new home. North America promised opportunities, work, and freedom.

Arrival Ordeal

As soon as they arrived in the port cities along North America's east coast, the immigrants were examined for disease. Sick passengers were **quarantined**, and those who were incurable were forced to return to Poland. Healthy passengers were sent to immigration centers, such as New York City's Ellis Island, which opened in 1892. There, they waited in long lines to be questioned by government officials. Immigration officers often changed the Poles' names because they could not pronounce or spell them. Many immigrants also requested a name change upon entering North America. Only those Poles who satisfied the officials were allowed to enter the country. Thousands more were turned away and had to return to their homeland.

▲ An Ellis Island inspector checks the eyes of a newly arrived immigrant in the early 1900s. The lines of people were controlled by railings and wire fences.

Getting to North America was not easy. **Emigrants** had to travel across several countries in Europe to reach a seaport and then sail across the stormy Atlantic Ocean by ship. To pay for their trip, many Poles had to sell all of their belongings. Few families could afford to travel together. Men often went alone, and saved money to pay for the rest of their family's voyage.

The earliest Polish immigrants spent months crossing the Atlantic aboard crowded sailing ships. Many caught deadly diseases during the voyage. By the late 1800s, there were steamships making the journey in just two weeks. There was less disease and hunger on these steamships, but the poorest Poles were still crammed into the smelly hold, or steerage section. Many traveled with just a suitcase and the clothes on their back.

▶ This Polish mother and child passed through Ellis Island in 1905.

Eyewitness to History

ADAM LABODA moved to the United States in the 1890s as a teenager. He made a career for himself as a spinner of wool, and married a fellow Pole. Here, Adam remembers his journey to New York.

" I was born in the village of Zowisezbie, near Tarnow. I was the oldest son of nine boys and two girls, and we had a farm of about twenty American acres (our acres equaled two and three-quarters of those here). My family lived in a two-room house, like a log cabin, with a straw thatched roof, a great brick stove for heat, and an iron range for cooking.

Our life on the farm was not easy, but it was not too harsh. We lived comfortably by all working together, our family. But I had an uncle in Syracuse, who wrote us about America, and so a party of fourteen boys from around our village was made up, with a man for a leader, to go to America.

We took a train and traveled two days to Bremen. There, we took a ship and voyaged for twelve days. The boys were all from fourteen to sixteen years of age. This was in the great emigration period from 1890 to about 1902. I remember we landed in New York Harbor on April 2, and then went up the river to Albany on another boat, and took the train to Gilbertsville, Massachusetts, where there are big woolen mills. I had a friend there and I got a job in the spinning room. "

Polonia

Most of the millions of Poles who came to North America between the 1870s and the beginning of World War I went to the United States. They took factory jobs in the cities of the northeast and midwest. The Polish community that formed in these regions is known as "Polonia."

Most of the Poles who came to North America during the late 1800s and early 1900s were farmers. About 110,000 Poles went to Canada. They settled on farms in the prairies and found work in Winnipeg or in the mines of northern Ontario. About 2.6 million Poles settled in the United States. They took up new trades in the factories of cities such as Buffalo, Chicago, Cleveland, Detroit, Milwaukee, and Pittsburgh.

▲ This store in the heart of Chicago's Polish Village sells books and magazines written in the Polish language.

Soon, the name Polonia was used to describe the growing Polish community made up of these immigrants. Polonians labored hard to earn their living. Any education beyond basic reading and writing was viewed as a luxury. Immigrants' children often left school at an early age to find work and help support their families.

Fearing that their traditional culture would disappear in Poland, many Polonians vowed to keep their language, customs, and religion alive in their new land. Many hoped to return to Poland one day, once they saved enough money to start their own business, or when the harsh rule of Poland's enemies came to an end. Polonians were slow to accept the English language and American customs because they lived and worked apart from English-speaking Americans.

▶ Mr Krukowski, a Polish settler, moved his house from one part of Alberta to another in 1927— by horse!

Most Polonians stayed within their own towns and neighborhoods, which they made to look and feel like those back in Poland. They set up their own Roman Catholic churches and founded schools to teach Polish language and history. Polonians formed charity groups, such as the Polish Union of America in 1889 and the Polish Women's Alliance in 1898, to help each other and fellow Poles overseas.

Polonia remained strongly Polish for many decades, but its members gradually adopted more of the cultures around them. Today, Polonian organizations still focus on promoting community pride, helping one another, and teaching about the Poles' contribution to North America.

▼ During World War I, nurses from Polish communities sailed from New York to help the wounded.

Polish White Cross
for the
Polish Army in France

A New Poland

Thousands of Poles from North America fought in World War I, in the hope of freeing their homeland: Poland. As part of the peace treaty that ended the war, much of the land that had been overtaken by the Prussians, Austrians, and Russians in the late 1700s was given back, and Poland once again became a nation. This happy event encouraged hundreds of thousands of Poles in the United States and Canada to move back to Poland after World War I.

Finding Work

During the largest wave of Polish immigration, Poles found jobs in North American factories, mines, lumberyards, and on farms. Men and women worked long hours for little pay, sometimes in unsafe conditions. Some fought prejudice in their workplace and communities.

▼ This happy Polish couple, photographed in 1940, developed waste land in Connecticut Valley. They chose to grow tobacco; other Poles planted crops of potatoes or onions.

Once Polish immigrants safely arrived in their new land, they were anxious to start earning a living. Many who knew agriculture moved to the countryside, where they took jobs as laborers. Others headed for the frontier and cleared land for their own farms. Poles became known for turning barren, abandoned land into profitable **land holdings**. In Canada, thousands of Poles rode the new railroad west to the prairies to set up farms and towns.

About two-thirds of Polish immigrants, including many former farmers, decided to stay in the cities. Industry boomed in the 1800s, and there was a constant demand for factory labor. Like many other immigrants at the time, most Poles had no special skills to offer. The fact that newcomers spoke little or no English was a further challenge to finding good jobs. As a result, most Poles were forced to take some of the hardest, most dangerous, and lowest-paying work.

Throughout the 1800s and into the 1900s, prejudice also worked against the Poles and kept them from gaining better jobs. Some employers did not hire them because they thought Poles were unintelligent and rowdy, or likely to break the law. Poles were sometimes passed over for jobs because English-speaking employers found their names difficult to pronounce. Like many **minority groups**, the Poles also suffered cruel, insulting jokes.

Despite such prejudice, Poles proved themselves to be hardworking and honest. Across the continent, they worked hard at a variety of jobs in **packinghouses**, sawmills, and lumberyards. The steelworks of the Chicago area attracted many Poles, and, in Detroit, Polish workers took jobs on the **assembly lines** of early automobile plants. Jobs in coal and iron mines brought workers west, as did **construction** of the railroads. While Polish men worked in heavy industry, women took on demanding jobs of their own in light industries such as textiles.

▲ **Many Poles found work on car assembly lines, such as this one in Detroit, Michigan.**

A Long Road to Success

After working in North America for many years, Poles gained more respect in their workplaces. They won praise in industries such as the auto industry, which employed thousands of Poles who worked hard in car factories. Some began their own businesses, such as printing, or opened shoe repair shops, grocery stores, or bakeries. Many Poles still faced unsafe jobs, low wages, and prejudice. In the 1930s, Polish workers became active in trade unions and fought hard for workers' rights. To help new immigrants find work and learn English, and to offer one another support, many Poles became involved in their local church and community groups.

◄ **A bakery in Chicago caters to the city's Polish Village.**

Eyewitness to History

Polish American ANNA NOVAK was born around 1909 in Wisconsin. She was brought up in an orphanage and then found work as a meatpacker. Talking in the 1930s, she describes the terrible conditions in the packing factory.

" One thing you should see, the rash the girls get, those that have to handle poisoned pork. And the acids from cans, it just gets you so that you can't stand up. You don't know what's the matter with you, but work you can't, to save your life. Then it's so easy to catch cold: one girl working right next to another coughs and you know she can't turn around. She's got production to make on a line, and there you are. The whole table of girls will be coughing and sneezing over their work. A girl can't take time off on account of a cold. The company wouldn't let them and they can't lose all that pay, anyway.

Another thing, in our department we have two toilets for one hundred girls. You should see before we got the union — you could scrape the muck off the floor with a knife. We made them put in a new floor and they promised to give us some new lockers. So far, there are thirty lockers for one hundred girls. Well, we're on their necks all the time now.

When we want to eat we've got to go over by the lockers and they're right on top of these two stinking toilets. If you knew the smell! And girls have to eat there! I wouldn't have lunch there if I had to walk four miles for a cup of coffee. You can't imagine what the combination of toilets, and disinfectant, and cigarette smoke, and sweat, and **stockyards** smells like! "

World War II and its Aftermath

The 1900s was a very difficult century for the people of Poland. Their country was brutally conquered in 1939 by Germany, and, afterward, controlled by Soviet Russia. Hundreds of thousands more Poles left their homeland, many fleeing for their lives.

Following World War I (1914–1918), Poland again became an independent country, and thousands of Poles moved back to their homeland from overseas. Poland's independence did not last long. In 1939, the leaders of Germany invaded Poland, which was the beginning of World War II. Members of the Polish government fled Poland. German rule, which lasted until 1944, was the worst in Polish history, and was to blame for the deaths of millions of Poles. The leader of Germany, Adolf Hitler, and his followers, called the Nazis, encouraged people to believe that ethnic minorities, in particular Jewish people, were to blame for poverty and crime. These people were forced to go to slave-labor camps in Poland and Germany where most of them were murdered. This act of mass execution is called the Holocaust.

About six million Poles were killed during World War II, and more than three million of them were Jewish.

▼ Hitler and his troops marched into Danzig, Poland, in September 1939. The banner across the street is written in German. It says: "Danzig welcomes its *Führer!*" Führer means leader.

When the war was finally over, tens of thousands of Poles came to North America. They were leaving the awful living conditions in their war-torn land. Many of these refugees were Jews and urban Poles who had good educations and jobs in the cities before the war. Large cities such as New York and Toronto became major destinations for the Polish Jews who survived the Holocaust. They found jobs and rebuilt their lives. The new Polish immigrants had little in common with Polonians, and did not **associate** with them.

In the years following World War II, Poland became a **Communist** country and was largely controlled by Russia, which led the Soviet Union, until 1991. Many Poles felt that the Communist leaders did not listen to what the people wanted. A group of politicians began a movement they called Solidarity. They staged strikes and voiced Polish people's desires for more political and religious freedom. In 1989, the Communists were removed from power and Poland was free once more.

▲ **German troops rounded up Poles and sent them to slave-labor camps.**

Recent Times

The people of Poland have enjoyed many freedoms since their country broke away from Soviet Russia in 1991, including the freedom to migrate. The latest wave of Polish immigrants have left their homeland for several reasons. Some joined family overseas, or were attracted by job opportunities in North America that did not exist in Poland. Others moved to escape poor living conditions. Although the Polish government has taken steps to improve these conditions, many Poles have decided to leave and start over elsewhere, rather than wait for social improvements that could take many years.

▼ **Lech Walesa led the trade union, Solidarity, which campaigned for Polish workers' rights in the 1980s.**

The Roman Catholic Church

For centuries, the Roman Catholic Church has played an important role in Polish history and culture. Polish immigrants brought this heritage with them to North America. Today, Roman Catholicism remains an important part of Polish American and Polish Canadian life at home and in the community.

For most Polish immigrants in North America, Roman Catholic practices were part of everyday life. Poles attended Church services on Sundays and on religious holidays, and tried to live according to the teachings of their local priest, or church leader. Family and public celebrations, including festivals, plays, and picnics, were all hosted by the neighborhood church. Priests were respected, powerful leaders within Polish communities.

▲ The Roman Catholic Church organized youth camps where children from Polish communities gathered for activities and fellowship.

In the centuries that Poland was controlled by foreign powers, the Church was one of the only places where Poles could practice their customs and language. In the same way, Polish immigrants in North America turned to the Roman Catholic Church, as they struggled against poverty, prejudice, and the hardships of living in an unfamiliar land.

◀ Pictures of the Black **Madonna** are popular in Polish American homes. The original, in Czestachowa, Poland, is a dark portrait of the Virgin Mary, in front of which people claim to have seen miracles.

The Church held Polish communities together. Immigrants established their own **parishes**, where Polish was spoken in church. They also established Polish Roman Catholic schools. The Roman Catholic Church even helped end prejudice against the Poles by electing a Pole, Karol Wojtyla, to be its leader in 1978. Wojtyla took the name Pope John Paul II, and made many North Americans aware that Poles deserve attention and respect.

Today, the Church is no longer always at the center of their lives but many Polish Roman Catholic families still gather at their local church to observe important **sacraments** throughout their lives. The sacraments of **baptism**, first **communion**, and **confirmation** welcome children into the Church. After each of these ceremonies, the child's family gathers at home to eat special foods and celebrate their experience.

In their homes, Polish North Americans often display signs of their Roman Catholic beliefs. They hang **crucifixes** and portraits of Jesus Christ, the Virgin Mary, and Pope John Paul II on the walls.

▲ This sign, in a house in Poletown, Detroit, Michigan, is in Polish. It says: "God Bless Our Home."

▼ Polish Canadian girls at their confirmation in 1940. Traditionally, children wore white for their confirmation, as a sign of purity.

Polish Culture

Despite the hardships they have faced as a people, the Poles are known for their love of joyful music and dance, rich foods, and beautiful folk art.

The rich culture that the Poles worked so hard to preserve in North America can be seen whenever Polish Americans or Canadians get together. It is not unusual to hear Polish spoken between family and friends at a gathering, nor for there to be traditional music, food, and handmade decorations.

It is difficult to think of Polish music without thinking of Polish dance. Both are major parts of Polish celebrations. The best known Polish dances are the polonaise and the polka. The polonaise, whose name means "Polish," is a very stately dance. The polka originated with the Czech people, but became very popular throughout Europe in the mid-1800s. The Poles loved it so much that they have played and danced to it ever since. A typical polka band is made up of singers, an accordion, drums, bass, and horns. Today, many Polish American and Polish Canadian polka bands tour throughout North America.

Poles also have great respect for Polish composers of religious and classical music, such as Karol Szymanowski, and Frederic Chopin. Chopin loved the folk melodies of his homeland and worked them into many of his compositions.

▲ Chopin wrote mainly for the piano. His works include the *Polonaise-Fantaisie* of 1845–1846.

▶ Dancers at the Polish Festival in Holmdel, New Jersey, wear colorful, traditional Polish costume.

Perhaps the most famous Polish woman was Maria Sklodovska (1867–1934), better known as Marie Curie. She and her French husband, Pierre, were awarded the Nobel Prize for Physics in 1903. In 1911, Marie was awarded a second Nobel Prize, for Chemistry.

Through years of poverty and struggle, many Poles learned to make good meals from whatever food was available. For this reason, many traditional dishes are made with cabbage, which was plentiful and stayed fresh a long time. Favorites include *sauerkraut* which is pickled cabbage and *golabki*, or cabbage rolls stuffed with meat. Polish food has a huge variety of dishes from hearty stews and *borscht*, or beet soup, to crunchy dill pickles and sweet *szarlotka*, which is an apple cake.

Two of the most famous Polish foods are *pierogi* and *kielbasas*. *Pierogi* are made from small pieces of dough, which are stuffed with potato and cheese, or *sauerkraut*. They are boiled, fried, and then served with sour cream. *Kielbasas* are smoked sausages seasoned with garlic and spices.

▲ Strings of tasty Polish sausages hang for sale in this Chicago butcher's store.

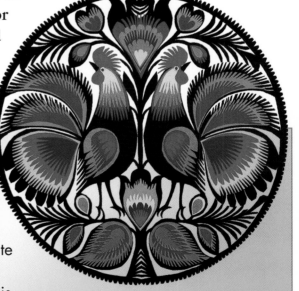

▲ Traditional *wycinanki* patterns include farm animals, flowers, woodland scenes, and birds.

Polish Paper Art

The art of *wycinanki* is just one of many traditional Polish folk arts practiced today in Poland and North America. *Wycinanki* are delicate paper cutouts made from very thin paper, they are used to decorate homes or the covers of books. It is said that beautiful *wycinanki* were once made with sheep shears by peasants in the 1800s to brighten their walls. Other popular folk arts include wood sculpture and *hafty*, or embroidery.

Polish Celebrations

Polish music, dance, food, and folk arts are all common parts of family and community celebrations. Poles in North America mark many religious and national holidays each year with parties and parades.

Each month of the Polish calendar is filled with fun events. Many Polish celebrations observe Roman Catholic holy days, while others honor important dates in Polish history, traditional harvest holidays, and birthdays.

Easter Sunday, which honors Christ's return to life after he was put to death, is an important Christian holiday. To prepare for Easter Sunday, people decorate *pisanki*, or Easter eggs with very elaborate and beautiful designs. During the Easter Sunday feast, family members give each other an egg. They compete to see whose egg has the toughest shell by knocking together the *pisanki*.

▲ **The annual Pulanski Day Parade in New York celebrates Polish American heritage.**

▼ **Polish Americans exchange decorated eggs called *pisanki* at Easter. Eggs are a symbol of new life.**

Polish Weddings

Polish weddings are marked with many old customs meant to bring good luck and health, happiness, and plentiful food to the newlyweds. One such custom is for parents to sprinkle the bride and groom with holy water before they leave for the church. After the wedding ceremony, the parents traditionally present them with bread, salt, and, sometimes, wine. Then the family and guests gather for a large dinner, followed by joyous dancing and singing that continue long into the night.

▲ **A Polish bridal party poses for a wedding photograph, in Chicago, in 1910. Later, the bride and groom settled in southern Alberta, Canada.**

Other Easter customs include taking foods such as eggs, ham, and kielbasas to church to be blessed by the priest. After attending church services on Easter morning, Polish families return home to feast. Among the many rich dishes, a small lamb made of butter or sugar is set out on the table, as a symbol of Christ.

An unusual Polish Easter tradition is called *Dyngus* or *Smigus*. On the Monday after Easter, boys are allowed to soak girls with water. In return, on Tuesday, girls have their chance to throw water over the boys!

There are many traditional Polish customs at Christmas, when Christians celebrate the birth of Jesus Christ. The most important is the *Wigilia*, a dinner held on December 24, the day before Christmas. As the sun sets, children watch for the first evening star to appear, the signal for the *Wigilia* feast to begin.

The family starts by sharing the *oplatek, or* bread wafer, and exchanging heartfelt wishes for their loved ones in the year to come. Then, everyone eats a lot of delicious food. Up to thirteen courses, all meatless, are served. Next, families exchange gifts. Many Polish children receive their gifts from *Swiety Mikolaj*, the Polish name for Santa Claus. Afterward, they go to church and sing *kolendy*, or Polish Christmas carols.

▼ **Nativity scenes decorate Polish churches and homes during Advent, the four weeks that lead up to Christmas Day.**

Here to Stay

Poles and their descendants have made many great achievements in North America, in fields ranging from the arts and sciences to industry and sports.

▲ **Thaddeus Kosciusko helped to win the Battle of Saratoga in 1777.**

Two of the earliest Poles to rise to fame in North America were Thaddeus Kosciusko and Casimir Pulaski. Both were military officers who left Europe after they were defeated fighting Poland's enemies. Kosciusko and Pulaski enlisted against the British in the War of Independence (1775–1783) and became heroes. Today, both men are honored with monuments. Pulaski is remembered each October with parades in New York and other cities.

Casimir Gzowski was an unknown engineer who came to North America in 1837. He helped build several railways, bridges, and canals in New York and Ontario that improved trade for both Canada and the United States. He built the first international railway line between Canada and the United States as well as a bridge across the Niagara River that connected Fort Erie, Ontario and Buffalo, New York. Casimir Gzowski also cared about the environment around him. He helped create a public park at Niagara Falls to preserve the beauty of the falls. In 1888, the Canadian Prime Minister honored him for his contributions to Canada and he became known as Sir Casimir Gzowski.

◄ **From left to right, Samuel, Harry, Jack, and Albert Warner, founded the movie company Warner Brothers. Their father, a poor shoemaker, left Poland for the United States in the late 1800s.**

◄ Harvey Keitel has appeared in more than 50 Hollywood movies. Here, he plays a cigar store owner in the 1995 film, *Smoke*.

Many Poles and their descendants have become entertainers. Harvey Keitel is one of many North American actors of Polish descent. Poles have also excelled on the business side of the film industry. Harry, Albert, Sam, and Jack Warner moved to Hollywood in 1918 and founded Warner Brothers, one of today's major movie studios. Another movie studio, Metro-Goldwyn-Mayer, or M.G.M., was co-founded by Polish-born Samuel Goldwyn.

Casimir Funk was one of many Polish scientists who came to North America. He discovered several vitamins, and showed how they prevent scurvy and rickets. Maria Goeppert Mayer was a nuclear physicist who came from Katowice, which became part of Poland after World War II. She shared the 1963 Nobel Prize in Physics for her studies of the atom.

▼ Wayne Gretzky played ice hockey for Canada against the United States in the Winter Olympics, 1998.

The Great Gretzky

Wayne Gretzky, who has Polish ancestors, is perhaps the greatest hockey player of all time. He retired in 1999 after twenty years with the National Hockey League. In that time, he set or tied 61 records, including those for the most goals, assists, and points. Gretzky was signed to the Edmonton Oilers in his late teens. After winning several Stanley Cups with that team, he went on to play for the Los Angeles Kings, St. Louis Blues, and New York Rangers. In his success, Gretzky joins other famous athletes of Polish descent, including baseball great Stan "The Man" Musial.

Glossary

allies Countries that have agreed to support each other.

ancestry Family line going back in time.

assembly line A line of machines and workers performing small jobs in order to put together a product.

associate To connect or keep company with.

baptism A ceremony involving water, as part of an initiation into the Christian church.

campaigned Fought for.

Christianity The religion of those who follow the teachings of Jesus Christ and the Bible.

colony Area of land settled or conquered by a distant state and controlled by it.

communion Receiving bread and wine in church, to symbolize the body and blood of Jesus Christ.

Communist Following communism, a system of government where there is no privately-owned property.

confirmation The service that makes someone a full member of the Roman Catholic Church, usually at the age of about nine.

construction Building.

convert To change from one religion to another.

crucifix A cross, such as the one on which Jesus Christ died.

culture A group of people's way of life, including their language, beliefs, and art.

czar A Russian king.

descendant A family member, such as a child, or grandchild.

disembark To get on to land from a ship.

emigrant Someone who leaves their own country to go and live in another one.

executed Put to death.

immigrate To come to settle in one country from another country.

Judaism The religion of the Jews, who follow the teachings of a holy book called the Torah.

land holding Land that is owned by a person.

literacy Reading and writing.

Madonna One of the names for Jesus Christ's mother, Mary.

minority groups A group regarded as different from the larger group of which it is a part.

misdemeanor A crime.

packinghouse A place where animals are slaughtered for meat, and where meat is processed.

parish A neighborhood that is looked after by a single priest.

Pope The head of the Roman Catholic Church.

prejudice An unfair opinion.

preserve To keep the same.

provisions Supplies of food and materials.

quarantined Kept away from other people, so that infectious diseases do not spread.

Roman Catholic Church The Christian church which is led by the Pope in Rome.

sacraments Religious rituals.

sentence Punishment for a crime.

stockyard Where livestock, such as cattle, are kept before they are slaughtered.

strike Refusal to work, in order to draw attention to unfair conditions.

subject Someone who is under the control of a king or ruler.

Index

1 2 3 4 5 6 7 8 9 0 Printed in the USA 5 4 3 2 1